DEAR DAD

Other Books by Bradley Trevor Greive

The Blue Day Book

The Blue Day Journal and Directory

Dear Mom

Looking for Mr. Right

The Meaning of Life

The Incredible Truth About Mothers

Tomorrow

Priceless: The Vanishing Beauty of a Fragile Planet

The Book for People Who Do Too Much

Friends to the End

The Blue Day Book for Kids

DEAR DAD

Father, Friend, and Hero

BRADLEY TREVOR GREIVE

**Andrews McMeel
Publishing**

Kansas City

05 06 07 08 09 TWP 10 9 8 7 6 5 4 3 2 1

ISBN: 0-7407-5024-0

Library of Congress Control Number: 2004111471

Book design and composition by Holly Camerlinck

Attention: Schools and Businesses:
Andrews McMeel books are available at quantity discounts with bulk purchase for educational, business, or sales promotional use. For information, please write to: Special Sales Department, Andrews McMeel Publishing, 4520 Main Street, Kansas City, Missouri 64111.

Photo Credits
Acclaim Images (USA)
www.acclaimimages.com
Alamy Images (UK)
www.alamy.com
Auscape International (Australia)
www.auscape.com.au
Austral International (Australia)
www.australphoto.com.au
Australian Picture Library (Australia)
www.australianpicturelibrary.com.au
BIG Australia (Australia)
www.bigaustralia.com.au
Dale C. Spartas
www.spartasphoto.com
Getty Images (Australia)
www.gettyimages.com
Photolibrary.com (Australia)
www.photolibrary.com
Photography E-biz (Australia)
www.photographyebiz.com.au
Richard du Toit
rdutoit@iafrica.com
Stock Photos (Australia)
www.stockphotos.com.au
Wildlight Photo Agency (Australia)
www.wildlight.com.au

Detailed page credits for the remarkable photographers whose work appears in *Dear Dad* and other books by Bradley Trevor Greive are freely available at www.btgstudios.com

I am forever proud
to be my father's ~~son~~ daughter

Acknowledgments

Following the release of my book *Dear Mom,* I received hundreds of warm, funny letters from readers asking for, nay, *demanding* a sequel for their dear dads. People clearly feel strongly about their fathers, and frankly, I was a little scared! This presented me with quite a challenge because I didn't know exactly how to write it—fathers and mothers are just different.

In the end, it has taken me more than three years, but now I am happy to have finally put down in words what I've wanted to say to my dad for a long time. I am very proud of this special little book. I believe my dad will like it, and I hope my readers are also pleased—especially those who are bigger than me!

I offer sincere thanks to all my publishing partners throughout the world who, with my team at BTG STUDIOS in Australia, have enabled me to do what I love once again. I must make special mention of the one and only Christine Schillig, my "Manuscript Mother Bear," at Andrews McMeel Publishing. Chris and I have made a great team from the very beginning.

As with my previous books, *Dear Dad* is built on a bedrock of beautiful images. I am very grateful to the photographers who shared their genius with me, especially Richard Du Toit, who went to great pains to get his images all the way to Kansas City from a remote corner of South Africa. I encourage everyone interested in the photographers and photo libraries that have contributed to my work to seek out their updated contact details at www.btgstudios.com.

In terms of father figures, I must pause to acknowledge my esteemed and benevolent literary agent, Sir Albert J. Zuckerman of Writers House, New York. My success as an author is entirely due to Al's fatherly guidance on life, literature, and inescapable leg-locks.

A few years back, we traveled together to South America to promote my books in Brazil. At a delicious luncheon in our honor, trouble broke out when a marmoset in a nearby tree, to whom I had been secretly throwing large red grapes, leaped through the window onto an unguarded fruit display and was sent into a furry frenzy by all the excitement and a belly buzzing with natural sugars. In the ensuing fracas, three waiters were bitten and scratched as was I and, regrettably, the president's wife, who also lost a priceless earring when she rolled clear of the snarling simian and the collapsing buffet.

Typically, Sir Albert kept his head, swiftly scooped up the tiny primate into a hollow melon, and bowled him between the legs of the presidential police to safety. In the time it took to gather ourselves, Al fashioned the first lady a replacement earring using his collectible Neil Diamond cufflinks and gently brushed the mango and papaya from her hair while humming the showstopper from Andrew Lloyd Webber's musical *Evita*—a most curious choice, I thought at the time.

When coffee and chocolates appeared, he took me aside to bandage my wounds with safety pins and napkins. "You know, Bradley," he chuckled with a pin between his teeth, "This reminds me of changing diapers on my kids and grandkids. No, not the smell, don't get me wrong! But I do look upon you as a son, a foolish monkey-feeding son, sure, but a son nonetheless, and today's messy drama brings back all the tough things about being a father that make the job so damn special. Raising a family is simply the sum total of everything that drives you crazy that you just can't live without. As a father, nothing, and I mean nothing, feels better than to be there for your child, no matter what. Perhaps one day, you'll understand what I mean."

I dream of the day, Al. I dream of the day.

DEAR DAD

My eyes are a lot younger than yours, Dad,
but I've still seen some pretty inspiring things in my time:

vast mountain ranges, majestic and timeless,

great sweeping thunderstorms
setting the heavens ablaze with their power,

and perhaps one or two neck-wrenchingly
enormous stacks of pancakes.

But if anything on this earth can hold me in total awe and admiration,
it has to be you, Dad. All my life I have looked up to you.

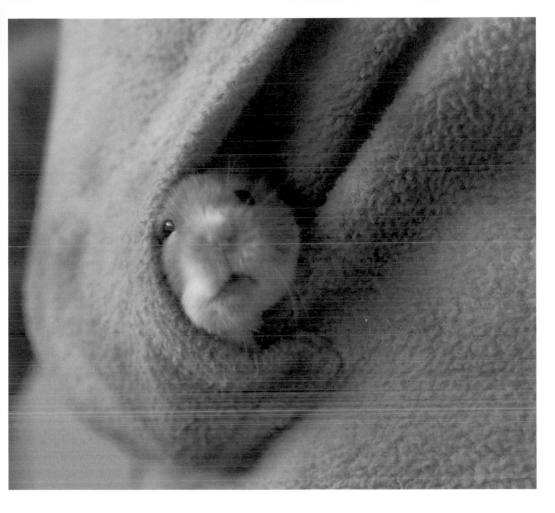

On the day my little bleary eyes first opened,
I raised them to the stars, and there you were,

an immovable tower of love and devotion.

In fact, my first and most precious memory of you is of an enormous, happy, laughing face staring lovingly down upon my own,

though I can't say your view was nearly as uplifting.

Upon reflection, I'm really not sure the whole "fatherhood" deal is as rosy as it is often made out to be.

However joyful the anticipation,
my arrival must have been something of a shock,

and I know I created plenty of anxiety. Mom was certainly worried about me, and you were worried about *both* of us.

I'll bet you asked yourself again and again how anything so small and helpless could bring about such drastic changes in your lives.

Along with a range of unexpectedly dramatic and
expensive consequences, you soon found yourself doing things
that simply don't feel natural for a man.

15

The truth is that new fathers find it far, far easier
to hold a football than a baby.

Work and family became a much more difficult balancing act,

and your role as provider got more and more demanding,

as did your duties as peacemaker and counselor.
You became the loving, tireless anchor
that holds fast to all that family means.

As you came to terms with these massive responsibilities,
I wonder how much you enjoyed my unceasing "Yak-Yak-Yak!"
in your ears, demanding your constant attention.

"Dad, watch me do five hundred jumping jacks."

"Daddy, Daddy, watch me burp the national anthem."

"Hey, Dad, watch me bury the house keys!"

In other words, I now realize that when I arrived on the scene,
you were stuck between a rock and, well, another rock.

24

That's why I am so grateful for your love, your courage,
your wisdom, and the benefits of all your hard work.
You gave me everything you had without a second thought.

Okay, maybe the odd "Hmmm,"
but no genuine second thoughts whatsoever.

Ultimately, I am me because I am part of you.
At the beginning, this probably wasn't too impressive.
I was a pretty feeble critter, quite funny looking,
often a bit stinky, and not exactly Einstein in diapers.

27

However, slowly but surely I have grown to be more and more like you in the very best ways.

I may not be an exact spitting image of you,

but we certainly appear alarmingly similar coming or going,
and I, for one, am really glad about that.

From the minute you woke me up in the morning

until you tucked me into bed at night,

your immense strength and gentleness
were molding me into the person I am now proud to be.

You taught me so much that I now take for granted:
how to tie up my shoes,

the importance of a firm handshake,

the not-so-subtle differences between boys and girls,

and in our rambling late-night conversations,
you even explained life, the universe, and why Mom
was entitled to go a little nuts every now and then.

When things didn't go quite as I'd hoped and planned,

I knew I could always count on you for a comforting hand
on my shoulder and words of encouragement.

You have always made me feel safe,

even when that meant putting yourself in harm's way. I know there's
nothing you wouldn't do to protect me from danger and distress.

And most important, you showed me how to stand up for myself and my beliefs when it mattered—nobody calls *me* "chicken"!

I'm sure you'd be the first to admit that our relationship wasn't always perfect. You snarled at me from time to time, though I almost certainly deserved worse.

I also endured "The Talk"

and "The Look."

Then there were your coma-inducing personal history lectures—
tedious and torturous tales about how everything
was so much harder when you were my age.

And as I was walking out the door for a fun night,
it was pretty annoying to hear you shout your parting words,
"Don't stay out late and don't get into any trouble!"

You always laughed way too loudly at your own weird jokes,

and somehow you always knew exactly
the worst possible time to walk into my bedroom,

or the bathroom,

or wander around the house in your oldest pair of underpants!

Of course, unpleasant as these particular memories are,
I'm really the one who should feel sheepish, because it's me
who needs to offer some apologies, not you, Dad.

I realize now that for a long time I was focused on only one thing:

me.

I can't imagine a reward big enough for all the times
you were stuck waiting to pick me up from school
or deliver me to practice or an outing with friends,

but I'll wager it wasn't turning around to see me
being violently carsick on your brand-new leather upholstery.

I also feel bad that I always seemed to be underfoot, getting in your way while you were trying to get something done—except, of course, when there were things you actually needed me to do.

No sir, nothing made me vanish from sight faster than the magic words
"Please go mow the lawn,"

or "How about giving me a hand with the dishes?"

On those occasions when I *did* do some work around the house,
my enthusiasm was such that jobs worth doing
were not necessarily done well.

Not that this stopped me from asking you for my allowance.

I feel embarrassed that you had to endure
millions of stupid questions as soon as I could talk.

"Dad, why does Grandma smell funny?"

64 "Daddy, why is your hair going gray and falling out?"

No matter what I asked, you would genuinely try to share
your hard-won wisdom and feed my curiosity with a rich,
rewarding answer, even if I was already distracted by something else.

Dad, when I have moments of seeing the world as you do,
I really admire the view. I am amazed at all you have achieved
and what you have helped me accomplish.

I realize I have been raised In the shadow of greatness.

I have walked beside an attentive giant,

and you have guided me gently but surely through my entire life.

So you see, Dad, that is why I will *always* look up to you.

But this is where it gets a little tricky,
because you're certainly not very good about accepting
overt displays of affection.

In fact, when it comes to emotional issues,
you're not always the easiest person to talk to, period.

Don't get me wrong—
it's not that you're the worst listener in the world,

it's just that communication with a father is, well, unique.
Sometimes it feels as if we even "speak" from the heart
without actually talking.

I know you've often said it's actions rather than words
that count the most,

but sometimes it does make me wonder, Dad,
if you really know how grateful I am for all you have done.

Are you as proud of me

as I am of you?

Do you have any idea how deeply I care about you?

One thing I've learned about life from you is just how fast it goes.
It may seem as if we have forever to explain how we feel,
then whooooooosh!

Suddenly, the opportunity has passed us by, and it's too late.

So Dad, if I could only say a few things just between you and me,
this is what I would want you to know.

Thank you for being the friend I could always turn to.

Thank you for being the hero I could always count on.

Thank you for being my father.

I love you, Dad.

The author being taught to wash behind his ears.
London, 1972.